TOTE BAG
17

SHOE BAG
8

LAUNDRY BAG
28

MAIN PHOTO: EMMA NOREN ; STEP-BY-STEP PHOTOS: JEMIMA SCHLEE

INSULATED BAG

Keep your picnic banquet chilled this summer in a practical but stylish insulated bag.
By Jemima Schlee

YOU WILL NEED

Yardage is based on 43"/44" wide fabric with a usable width of 40" for cotton fabrics and 58"/59" wide fabric for ripstop nylon fabric.

- $\frac{7}{8}$ yd of cotton print fabric for top
- $\frac{5}{8}$ yd of cotton print fabric for base
- $\frac{7}{8}$ yd of ripstop nylon fabric
- $1\frac{1}{4}$ yds of Insul-Bright™ thermal fabric
- $1\frac{1}{4}$ yds of $1\frac{1}{2}$" wide twill tape
- 1" "D" rings (optional)
- 19" heavyweight separating zipper
- Sewing machine
- Zipper foot
- Thread
- Sewing needles and pins
- Scissors
- Iron

CUTTING LIST:

Top fabric

Two $29\frac{5}{8}$" x 11" rectangles for bag top

Two $12\frac{3}{4}$" x $6\frac{3}{4}$" rectangles for pockets

Two 4" x $7\frac{7}{8}$" rectangles for zipper tabs

Base fabric

$29\frac{5}{8}$" x $20\frac{1}{2}$" rectangle for the base

Two 3" x 4" rectangles for side tabs (optional)

Ripstop nylon

$29\frac{5}{8}$" x $41\frac{1}{2}$" rectangle for the lining

Insul-Bright thermal fabric

$29\frac{5}{8}$" x $41\frac{1}{2}$" rectangle for bag interlining

Two $6\frac{3}{4}$" x $6\frac{3}{8}$" rectangles for pocket interlining

Two $1\frac{7}{8}$" x $7\frac{7}{8}$" rectangles for the zipper tabs

TO MAKE

Note: *Match right sides and raw edges and use a $\frac{1}{2}$" seam allowance unless otherwise indicated.*

1 To make handles, cut the tape into two 22" lengths. Fold each length in half (now $\frac{3}{4}$" wide) and stitch $4\frac{3}{4}$" in the center of the tape close to the edge, backstitching at beginning and end (*image 1*). Set these aside.

2 To make the pocket, match wrong sides and press pocket rectangle in half (now $6\frac{3}{4}$" x $6\frac{3}{8}$"); open it out again. Aligning it with the crease mark, place a thermal fabric pocket rectangle on one half of pocket rectangle. Stitch along the edge of the thermal fabric to hold it in position (*image 2*).

3 Fold the other half of the fabric over and sew two lines of topstitching $\frac{1}{8}$" and $\frac{3}{8}$" from the folded edge (*image 3*). Repeat Steps 2-3 to make the remaining pocket.

4 With the raw edges of one pocket matching the bottom edge and centered on the bag top, baste one pocket on the right side of the bag top (*image 4*).

5 Place ends of one handle $^{3}/_{8}$" over each side of the pocket; pin.

6 Topstitch along one edge of the handle to 2" above the top edge of the pocket. Stitch an "X" at the top to strengthen the handle. Stitch along the remaining edge to the bottom (*image 5*). Repeat on the opposite side of the pocket.

7 Repeat with the other bag top, pocket, and handle.

8 To make the outer bag sides, sew the two bag tops to the base (*image 6*). Press the seam allowances toward the base and topstitch $^{1}/_{8}$" and $^{3}/_{8}$" from the seam (*image 7*).

9 Aligning the top edges, place the outer bag on top of the bag interlining, right side up. Open the zipper. Place one half of the zipper face down and centered along the top and with the zipper teeth $^{7}/_{8}$" below the raw edge; baste. Aligning the top edges, place the lining on top, sandwiching the zipper in between; baste (*image 8*). Stitch along the top edge close to the zipper teeth.

10 Trim any excess thermal fabric and/or lining even with outer bag. Repeat Step 9 with the opposite top edge of the outer bag. Turn and press outer bag away from zipper; do not touch lining with iron.

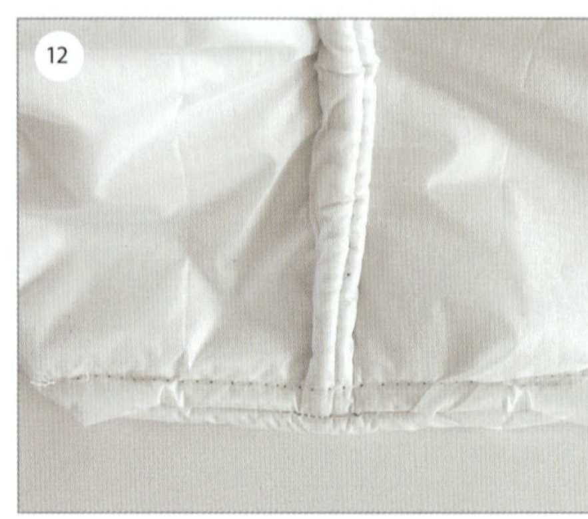

TIPS

- Stitch the zipper and seams using a zipper foot on your machine – it makes it easier to stitch through so many layers.
- When stitching through multiple layers of fabrics, take it slow. When the machine struggles, turn the wheel by hand to assist it through thick areas.

11 Optional: To make each side tab, match wrong sides and long raw edges and press side tab in half (now 1 1/2" x 4"); unfold. Press long edges to meet the center crease *(image 9)*. Refold and press again. Topstitch along each long edge of the tab.

12 Close the zipper. Matching **lining** sides, pin the bag together along the sides. Optional: Slip a "D" ring on one side tab. Matching raw edges, fold side tab in half. Pin the tab to the bag aligned with the top of the base; baste (*image 10*).

13 To taper the sides of the bag, mark a point along the top of the bag 2 3/4" from the top corner. Mark another point along one side of the bag 6 1/4" down from the top corner. Draw a line from point to point with a pencil. Repeat for the remaining side. Beginning at the bottom, stitch side seams. When you get to the first marks, follow the drawn lines to taper the sides. Trim the seam allowances to 1/4".

14 To make neatly finished seams, turn the bag **wrong** side out. Sew the bag together along the sides.

15 To box the bottom of the bag, match **wrong** sides and align side seam with bottom seam; stitch across the corner 4" from the point. Repeat for remaining corner of bag. Trim each corner 1/4" from the seam.

16 To make neatly finished seams, turn the bag **wrong** side out. Pin the bag together along the corners. Sew each corner seam *(image 12)*. Turn bag right side out.

17 To make a zipper tab, press long raw edges to wrong side 1". Slip one thermal fabric zipper tab under one fold. Fold the other side over to cover the thermal fabric and align the two folded edges. Pin and topstitch along each long edge (*image 13*). Repeat with remaining zipper tab.

18 Matching raw ends, fold one zipper tab in half. Zigzag stitch along the raw ends to reduce fraying. Pinching ends together, pin the zipper tab inside the bag 1 1/8" from top of one side seam. Stitch two vertical lines 1 1/8" long up either edge of the tab through all thicknesses of fabric, lining and thermal fabric, backstitching several times for strength (*image 14*).

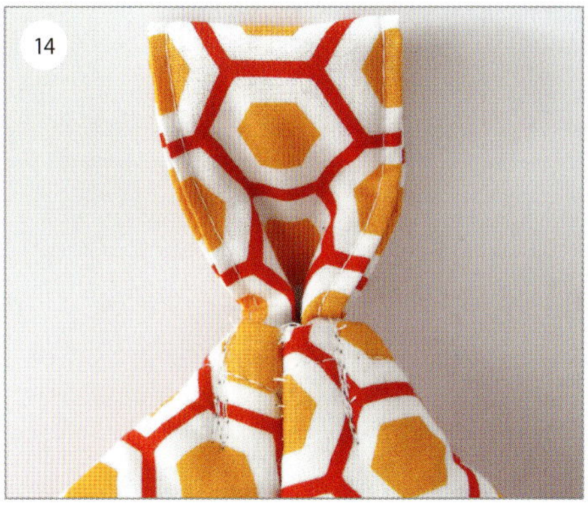

DENIM POCKET PURSE

Make a funky purse from pockets!
By Tansy Wilson

YOU WILL NEED

- Two denim pockets
- Fabric for lining
- Buttons or similar embellishments
- Thread in a complementary color
- Small zipper - Measure the top of the pocket and use a zipper as close to this length as possible. Our pockets are 6$^3/_8$" wide and we used a 7" zipper.

TO MAKE

***Note:** Match right sides and raw edges and use a $^1/_2$" seam allowance unless otherwise indicated.*

1 Remove any brads from pockets. Make sure that both pockets fit together when placed back to back, as some pockets are asymmetrical.

2 Using the pocket as a pattern, cut two lining pieces, adding $^1/_2$" on all sides for seam allowances.

3 Sew on any buttons or similar embellishments to make your purse really unique and personal. We added some mother of pearl buttons.

4 Keep the zipper closed. Aligning the top raw edge of the pocket lining with the edge of the zipper tape, pin the wrong side of one zipper tape to the right side of one pocket lining. Aligning the top edge of the pocket with the zipper teeth, pin one pocket to the right side of the same zipper tape (*image 1*). Sew along top of pocket. Repeat for the pocket and pocket lining on the opposite zipper tape.

5 To make the lining, keep the pockets out of the way and sew the lining pockets right sides together. Trim seam allowances to $^1/_4$".

6 Following the original stitching line on the pocket, match sides and stitch the pockets together.

7 Place the lining inside the pocket.

TIPS

- You can add a strap by cutting a strip of denim from the leg of the jeans, turning the purse into a small bag.
- Always keep the pins at a right angle to the stitching line as they are really easy to pull out when sewing rather than having to stop and lift the presser foot!

MAIN PHOTOGRAPHS: PETE JONES; STEP PHOTOGRAPHS: TANSY WILSON

SHOE BAG

Store your favorite shoes in perfect style.
By Jemima Schlee

PHOTOS: EMMA NOREN; STEP PHOTOS: JEMIMA SCHLEE

YOU WILL NEED

- $12\frac{1}{2}$" x 33" piece of cotton fabric for the outer bag
- $12\frac{1}{2}$" x 40" piece of cotton fabric for the lining
- $3\frac{1}{4}$" x 12" and $1\frac{3}{4}$" x 35" pieces of contrasting patterned fabric for the hanging loop and drawstring
- $5\frac{1}{2}$" x $7\frac{1}{2}$" piece of white cotton fabric for the photo transfer
- Digital camera
- Photo transfer paper
- Sewing machine
- Sewing threads to match all three colored fabrics
- Scissors
- Safety pin
- Iron

TO MAKE

***Note:** Match right sides and raw edges and use a $\frac{1}{2}$" seam allowance unless otherwise indicated.*

1. Take a photograph of a pair of shoes with the digital camera. Size the photo to $4\frac{1}{2}$" x $6\frac{1}{2}$", adjust the image (in this case from full color to sepia), and add a patterned frame, if you wish.

2. Follow the manufacturer's instructions to transfer the image onto the white fabric rectangle (do not touch iron to transfer). Turn all the edges $\frac{1}{2}$ to wrong side; baste.

3. Fold the outer bag fabric in half, right side out, to make a $12\frac{1}{2}$" x $16\frac{1}{2}$" rectangle. Center the photo panel $2\frac{1}{4}$" from the bottom fold. Pin in place close to the edge through top layer only. Unfold and topstitch close to the edge. Remove all basting and pins (*image 1*).

4 Fold the outer bag fabric right sides together and pin along the long edges. Mark a point $1\frac{1}{4}$" from the top edge on one side. Beginning stitching at mark, sew down both sides.

5 To finish the opening, press the seam allowances $\frac{1}{2}$" to wrong side along the side opening and stitch by machine close to the fold down one side, across the seamline, and up the other side of the opening to prevent fraying. Clip the corners of the outer bag; turn right side out.

6 Fold the lining in half, right sides together to make a $12\frac{1}{2}$" x 20" rectangle. Sew along the two long edges. Clip corners; do not turn right side out.

7 To make the hanging loop, match wrong sides and long raw edges and press hanging loop in half; unfold. Press long edges to meet the center crease. Refold and press again. Topstitch along each long edge of the loop.

8 Pressing the short edges of the drawstring $\frac{1}{4}$" to wrong side first, repeat Step 7 to make the drawstring (*image 2*), .

9 Matching right sides, slip the outer bag (right side out) inside the lining. Align the top edges and baste. At the same time, fold the hanging loop in half and center and align the raw edges on the top edge of the outer bag back, sandwiched the hanging loop in between (*image 3*). Stitch a 1" seam allowance all around, leaving a 2" opening to one side of the hanging loop for turning. Press the seam allowances towards the lining.

10 Turn the bag right side out through the opening. Push the lining into the bottom corners of the outer bag. This will create a "cuff" of the lining at the top of the bag. Press the top, ensuring that the seam allowance is pressed down, away from the top opening of the bag and that the hanging loop faces upward beyond the top edge (*image 4*).

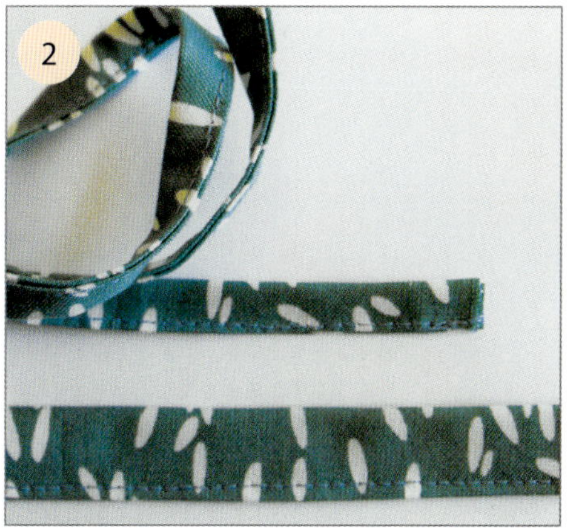

11 Topstitch close to the seam on the outer fabric side through all layers. Sew another row of stitching $\frac{1}{2}$" below the first, again stitching through all layers and thus creating a casing for the drawstring.

12 Feed the drawstring through the casing using a safety pin (*image 5*). Tie tight knots at each end of the drawstring to prevent it from pulling through the casing.

MAIN PHOTO: EMMA NOREN; STEP-BY-STEP PHOTOS: SUZANNE ROWLAND

GARMENT BAG

Sew a pretty and useful zip-up garment bag to travel in style.
By Suzanne Rowland

YOU WILL NEED

Yardage is based on 43"/44" wide fabric with a usable width of 40".

- $2^{1}/_{4}$ yds of medium weight fabric
- 6 yds of $^{7}/_{8}$" wide cotton double-fold bias tape
- 32" metal separating zipper
- Matching thread
- Sewing machine
- Iron
- Scissors
- Pins
- Fabric marker
- Curved ruler

TO MAKE

***Note:** Match right sides and raw edges and use a $^{1}/_{4}$" seam allowance unless otherwise indicated.*

1 Cut the following from fabric:
- bag back 24" x 40".
- two bag fronts 12" x 40".
- zipper top 2" x $3^{1}/_{2}$".
- zipper bottom 2" x 12".
- bottom loop 2" x 5".

2 To mark the rounded shape for the shoulders, fold the bag back in half lengthwise, decide which will be the top end and mark 7" down on the side. At the top, mark 2" from the fold. Using a curved ruler, join the two marks (*image 1*) and mark. Cut out along drawn line.

3 Use the bag back as a pattern for marking and cutting the same shape on the bag fronts.

4 Cut two 40" pieces of bias tape. Place the edge of the opened bias tape on the right side of the fabric along the long straight edge of one bag front. Pin in place and sew along the outer crease (*image 2*).

5 Press the tape to the wrong side. The other edge of the tape will remain unfolded. Baste in place (*image 3*). Repeat for remaining bag front.

6 To make the zipper bottom, match short raw edges and sew a $^{1}/_{4}$" seam allowance along each long side (*image 4*). Repeat to make the zipper top. Clip corners and turn each piece right side out; press.

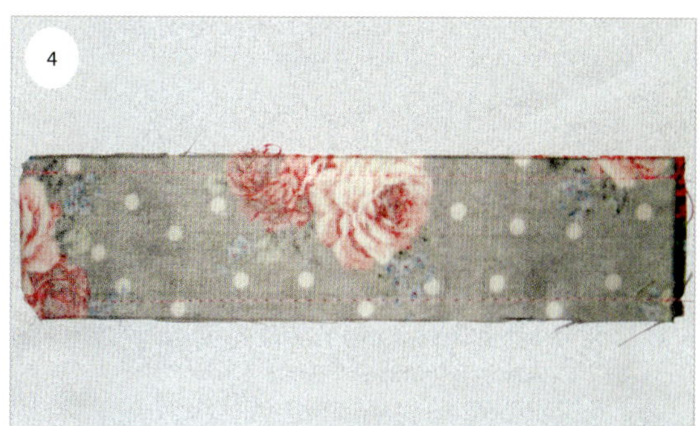

7 Aligning the raw edges, place the zipper top and zipper bottom under the bound edge of one front section.

8 Position the zipper in place under the bag front. Beginning at the top, pin and baste to secure (*image 5*).

9 Sew along the edge of the binding close to the fabric (not the edge nearest to the zipper teeth).

10 Repeat Steps 8-9 to attach the zipper to the remaining bag front (*image 6*).

11 To make the bottom loop, match long raw edges and sew a 1/4" seam allowance along the long raw edges. Turn right side out; press. Fold the loop in half and sew raw edges over the zipper bottom (*image 7*).

12 Repeat Steps 4-5 and use a 4" length of bias tape to finish off the center back edge.

13 Place the bag fronts and bag back together with wrong sides facing. Carefully match up all raw edges and trim to fit if necessary. Pin together and using the longest stitch on the machine, sew around the edge of the bag, leaving a 4" opening at the neck.

14 To bind the bag with bias tape, open the tape and place it around the side and top edges. Sew in the crease as before. Trim excess tape. Press the tape to the wrong side. Keep the other edge folded and pin and topstitch in place. Make sure you tuck the back neck into the binding when you are topstitching (*image 8*).

15 Add bias tape to the bottom edge in the same manner. Leave about 1/2" extra at each end to fold in and finish the corners (*image 9*).

16 Place a coat hanger in the bag and it's ready to go.

TIP

- It's easy to make this into a longer bag and would be ideal for storing a long dress. For a longer bag, you could use continuous zipper, available to buy by the yard.

TRAVEL BAG

No self-respecting traveler sets off without their trusty travel bag. Create your very own using vibrant oilcloth. By Emma Herian.

MAIN PHOTOS: EMMA NOREN; STEP-BY-STEP PHOTOS: EMMA HERIAN

YOU WILL NEED

Yardage is based on 43"/44" wide fabric with a usable width of 40".

- 3/4 yd of floral print oilcloth
- 3/4 yd of red solid oilcloth
- 2 3/4 yds of turquoise 7/8" wide double-fold bias tape
- 1 3/4 yds of 1" wide red cotton twill tape
- 12" pink zipper
- Tissue paper
- Thread
- Sewing machine
- Zipper foot

TO MAKE

***Note:** Match right sides and raw edges and use a 1/4" seam allowance unless otherwise indicated. See Tip on page 15 for sewing on oilcloth. Finger-press seams and folds; do **not** use an iron on oilcloth.*

1 Enlarge the pattern on page 16. Cut one travel bag from each fabric using the pattern. Set the red piece aside. For ties, cut two 20" pieces from red twill tape. Fold one end 7/8" to the wrong side and position 3/4" from the top on the right side of the floral print oilcloth. Sew a rectangle with an "X" in the middle (*image 1*). Repeat with the remaining length of twill tape but position it 7" from the bottom at the other end of the floral print oilcloth.

2 Cut the bottom pocket 14 1/2" x 6" from the floral print oilcloth. Cut a 15" length of bias tape. Insert the raw edge of the pocket into the folded bias tape. Sew along the folded edge (*image 2*). Trim ends of bias tape even with edges of pocket.

3 Fold a 3/8" hem along the bottom edge and at both side edges of the pocket. Center the pocket 1 1/8" from the bottom and 5/8" from the sides of the red oilcloth travel bag.

4 Fold a 3/4" tuck at each side; pin. Carefully sew along the base of the pocket which will secure the tucks; trim any threads.

5 From the red oilcloth, cut out the middle pocket 11 3/4" x 7 1/8" and the top pocket 11 3/4" x 9".

6 Fold top of middle pocket 1/2" to wrong side. Place the folded edge close to the zipper teeth on one zipper tape. Use the zipper foot to topstitch close to the folded edge. Fold the bottom edge of the top pocket 1/2" to wrong side. Place the folded edge close to the zipper teeth on the remaining zipper tape. Topstitch close to the folded edge. You should end up with a zipper that has two pieces of fabric sewn to either side, one larger than the other. These will form the middle zipper pocket and the top open pocket.

7 Sew a strip of bias tape along the top of the top pocket (the larger piece).

8 Fold the bottom edge of the middle pocket (smaller side of zipper piece) 5/8" to the wrong side. Place the pockets on the red oilcloth travel bag with the bottom edge about 9" from the bottom of the travel bag. Sew close to the side edges to hold the pockets in place.

9 Measure 8$^3/_4$" from the top edge of the travel bag (*image 3*). Placing a thin strip of tissue paper across the pocket at this point and beneath, sew across the pocket to form the top of the zipper pocket.

10 To make the top pockets above the zipper pocket, sew two vertical lines about 4" apart, backstitching at either end; trim the threads (*image 4*).

11 For hanger, cut a 5$^1/_2$" piece of red twill tape and pin into a loop at the center top of the floral print travel bag (*image 5*). Match wrong sides and place the red oilcloth travel bag with the pockets and the floral print travel bag together; pin all the way around the edge.

12 Starting at the bottom, insert the raw edge of the bag between the crease of the bias tape and topstitch all the way around (*image 6*). Make sure you have sandwiched all the edges, especially the pocket sides and the loop.

TIPS

- When sewing oilcloth, always place a piece of tissue paper on either side; this prevents the oilcloth from slipping under the sewing machine foot. Once sewing is finished, simply tear the paper away!
- Only pin around the edges where you will sew as this will hide the pin marks.

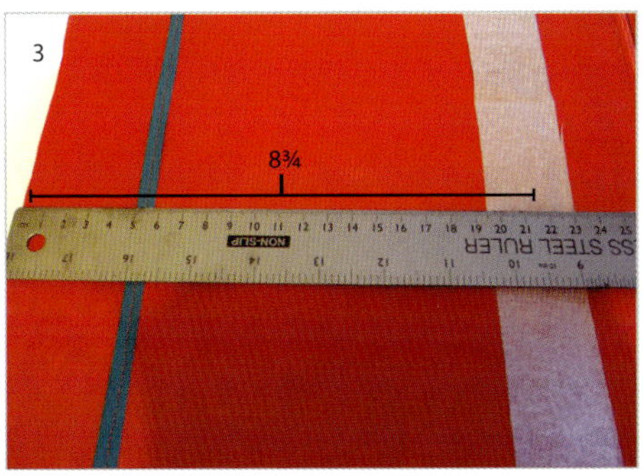

TRAVEL BAG (page 13)

Photocopy at 268% for actual size

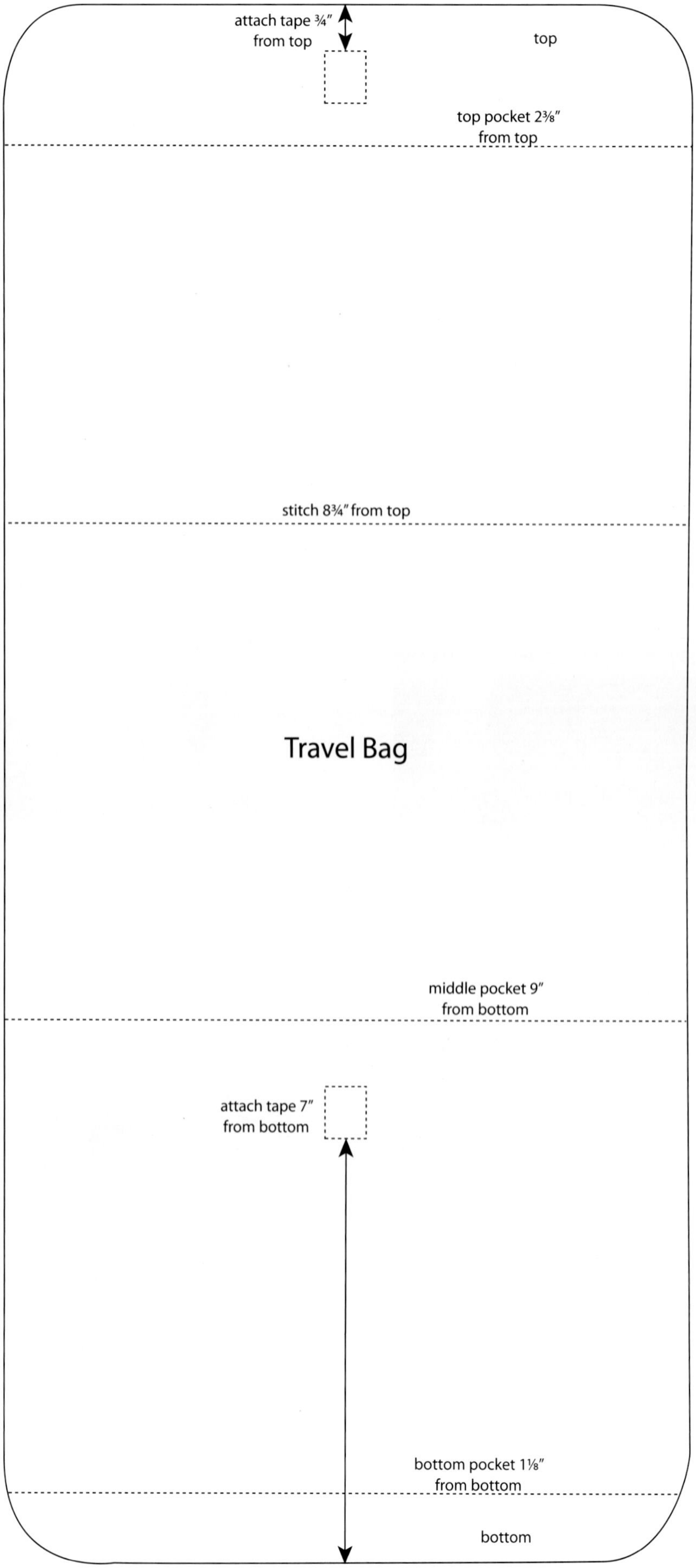

TOTE BAG

Make everlasting roses just by rolling, folding, and twisting strips of fabric and adorn a beautifully handmade simple linen bag – elegant with a romantic touch.
By Pascale Mestdagh

MAIN PHOTOS: EMMA NOREN; STEP-BY-STEP PHOTOS: PASCALE MESTDAGH

YOU WILL NEED

Yardage is based on 43"/44" wide fabric with a usable width of 40".

- 1/2 yard of heavy weight linen, cotton, or linen/cotton blend canvas for bag body
- 1/2 yard of light weight cotton fabric for lining
- Long pieces of fabric scraps (cotton muslin or poplin) at least 22" long for the flowers
- Two leather handles 1" x 18" each
- Threads
- Heavy duty thread
- Sewing machine
- Heavy duty sewing machine needle (100/16)
- Hand sewing needle
- Pins
- Scissors
- Binder clips
- Carbon dressmaker's tracing paper and tracing wheel

TO MAKE THE FABRIC ROSES

1. Tear strips of fabric. The width and length of the strips will determine the size of the flower. For a 2" diameter flower, use a strip 1 3/8" x 21 3/4". For a 1 3/8" diameter flower, use a strip 1" x 19 3/4".

2. Fold about 1" of the strip in half lengthwise with the fold facing up. Next, fold in a 45° angle as shown (*image 1*).

3. Start rolling the fabric to form the flower center (*image 2*).

1

2

4 Continue to roll but, as you go, fold and twist the strip in a slight angle to form the petals (*images 3 and 4*). Keep wrapping the fabric in this manner, folding and twisting as you go.

5 When you've reached the end of the strip, stick a few pins through the base of the flower to hold everything in place (*image 5*).

6 Thread a sewing needle with matching thread. Secure everything with a few small stitches through the base of the flower making sure to go through all layers of fabric (*image 6*). Remove the pins.

TIPS

- Wash the linen prior to cutting. Not only will it remove any residue left from the manufacturing process, but it will also make the fabric softer and enhance its natural luster as well as accounting for any shrinkage.
- Linen tends to fray; use a zigzag stitch to finish the raw edges of the seams.
- For a festive look, make the flowers in satin, silk or lightweight velvet and use them to adorn a dress or jacket or attach them to a headband or hairpin.

TO MAKE THE BAG

Note: *Match right sides and raw edges and use a 1/2" seam allowance unless otherwise indicated.*

1 Enlarge the pattern pieces on page 21. Seam allowances are included unless stated otherwise (notably at the facing cutting line where 1/2" needs to be added).

2 From the bag body fabric, cut two bag bodies and two facings (adding 1/2" seam allowance at the bottom of the facing cutting line). From the lining fabric, cut two bag bodies (adding a 1/2" seam allowance at the top of the facing cutting line) and one pocket 7 3/4" x 9 1/2". Transfer darts and the position of the handles onto the wrong sides of the bag fabric using transfer paper and a tracing wheel. Transfer the darts and position of the pocket onto the wrong sides of the lining fabric.

3 To make the pocket, press a double 1" hem on one short end. Pin and machine stitch. Press a 1/2" hem on the other three sides (*image 7*). Pin the pocket into place on the lining and topstitch along the side and bottom edges.

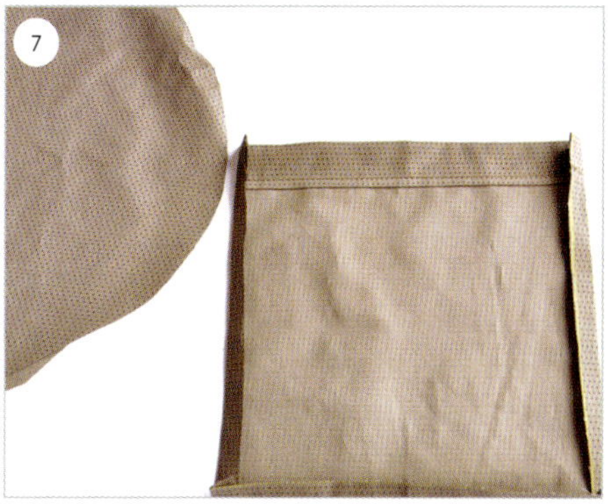

4 To make the darts in the lining, fold the fabric on the wrong side of the fabric as marked. Pin together and machine stitch. Repeat for the darts in the bag body; press.

5 To make the lining, sew one facing strip to top of one lining piece; press. Repeat for the remaining lining and facing. Topstitch on the facing, near the seam using a long stitch setting. Aligning the darts, sew the bag body lining/facing pieces together, leaving a 4"-6" opening at the bottom for turning (*image 8*). Turn the lining wrong side out; press.

6 To make the bag body, sew the bag body pieces together, aligning the darts. Turn bag body right side out; press.

7 Arrange the fabric flowers on one side of the bag body, staying approximately 1" below the top edge (*image 9*). Hand sew each flower to the bag body.

8 Place the handles along the top edge of the bag body as marked on the pattern, making sure they're not twisted. Hold in place using binder clips (*image 10*). Using a heavy-duty sewing machine needle and heavy duty thread, baste handles to bag body about 1/2" from the raw edge.

9 Place the bag body inside the lining, aligning the seamlines (so right sides of the fabric are matching); pin (*image 11*). Make sure the handles are sandwiched in between both layers. Sew together using a 5/8" seam allowance.

10 Turn the bag right side out through the opening in the lining. Sew the opening closed (*image 12*). Shape the bag, aligning the seams; press, being careful not to touch the leather handles with the iron. Topstitch near the edge using a long stitch.

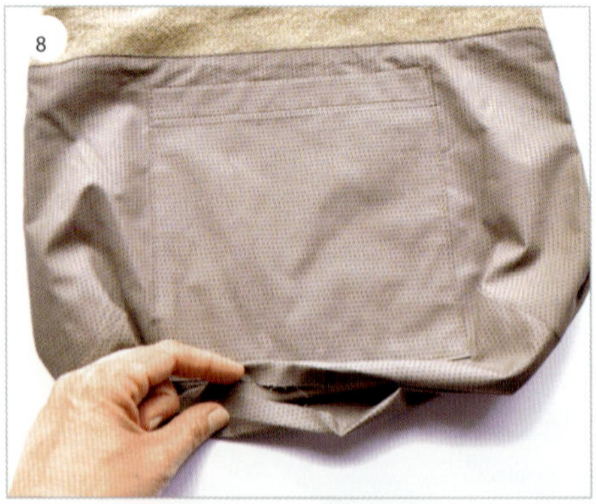
8

9

10

11

12

TOTE BAG (page 17)

Photocopy at 164% for actual size

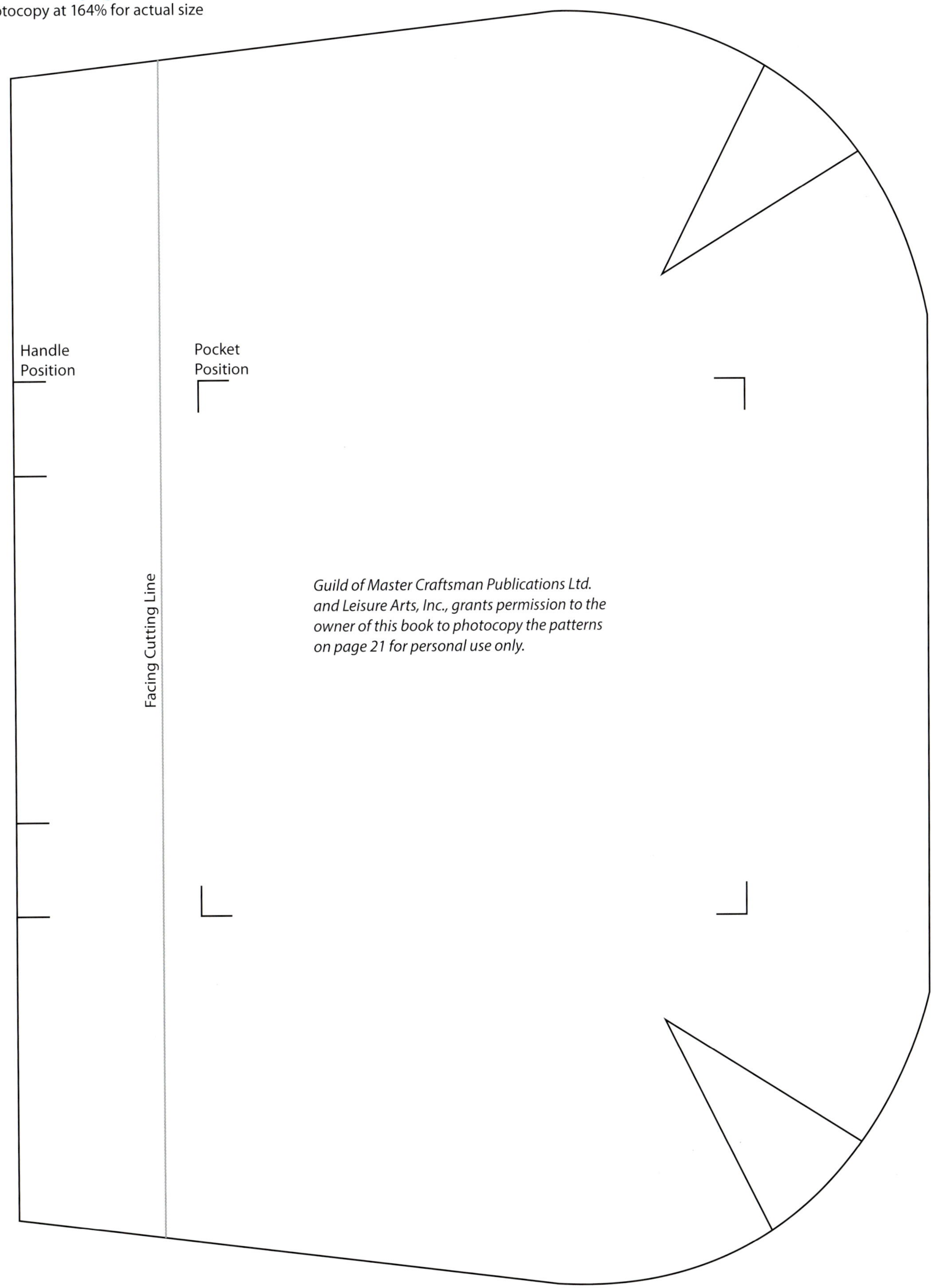

MAIN PHOTO: EMMA NOREN; STEP-BY-STEP PHOTOS: JEMIMA SCHLEE

MAKEUP BAG

Snap open a plain linen purse to reveal a rich patterned interior.
By Jemima Schlee

YOU WILL NEED

- 8" x 15 3/4" plain linen for bag body
- 8" x 15 3/4" floral fabric for lining
- 8" x 15 3/4" heavyweight sew-in interfacing
- 5" glue-in purse frame
- Threads to match the fabrics
- Scissors
- Sewing needle and pins
- Iron
- E6000® industrial strength adhesive

TO MAKE

***Note:** Match right sides and raw edges and use a 1/2" seam allowance unless otherwise indicated.*

1 Cut two purse pieces from the bag body fabric, lining fabric, and interfacing using the pattern on page 25.

2 Backstitching at the beginning and end and leaving a 2 3/4" opening for turning along the bottom, sew the lining pieces together between the dots. Press the seam allowances open.

3 To box the bottom of the lining, match right sides and align side seam with bottom seam; stitch across the corner 1" from the point (*image 1*). Repeat for remaining corner of lining. Trim each corner 1/4" from the seamline. Turn the lining right side out.

4 Place the two pieces of bag body fabric together. Sandwich them between the two pieces of interfacing; pin. Backstitching at the beginning and end, sew all four layers together between the two dots (*image 2*).

5 Repeat Step 3 to box the bottom of the bag body (*image 3*).

6 Make a clip in both the bag body and the lining where the stitching starts and stops.

TIP

- When sewing different fabrics together, fill the bobbin with a different color to the one you thread the machine with so that any topstitching is as invisible as possible.

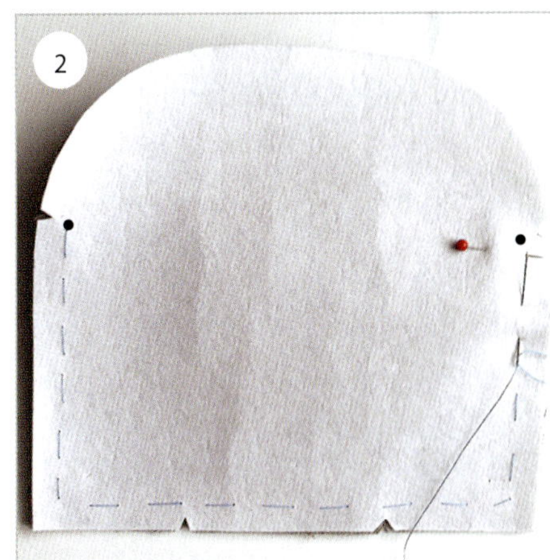

7 Place the lining inside the bag body (which is still wrong side out) and align all the edges and the side seams; pin (*image 4*).

8 Starting at the top center of one side, sew one bag body to one lining. Sew all the way around to the opposite bag body and lining – stop at the side seams with the needle down, raise the foot and manipulate the work under it so that you can continue without breaking the stitching.

9 Clip the curved edge (*image 5*).

10 Carefully turn the purse right side out through the opening (*image 6*). Stitch the opening closed and press so that you have a good crisp edge all around the top opening (*image 7*). Topstitch close to the edge.

11 Place a line of adhesive along the inside of one half of the frame, starting and stopping about 3/4" from the hinge at either side. Do the same along one side of the purse opening, starting and stopping 1/2" from each side seam. Insert the fabric into the frame, making sure that the sides are even first and then feeding the center in. Use your fingers or a sharp-pointed object to push the fabric in and make sure that the line of topstitching is hidden (*image 8*). Allow to dry completely before gluing the other side.

4

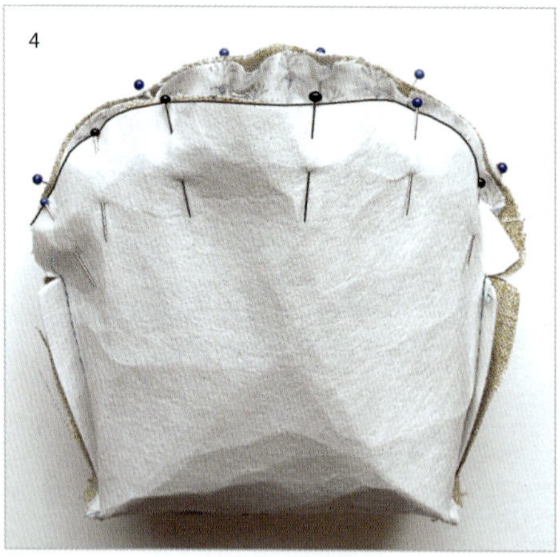

5

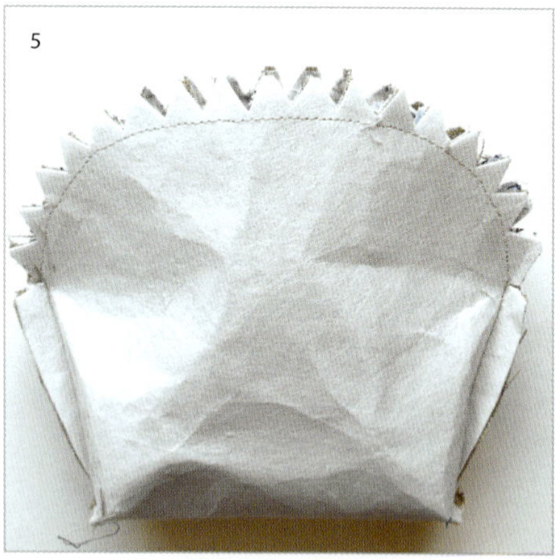

6

7

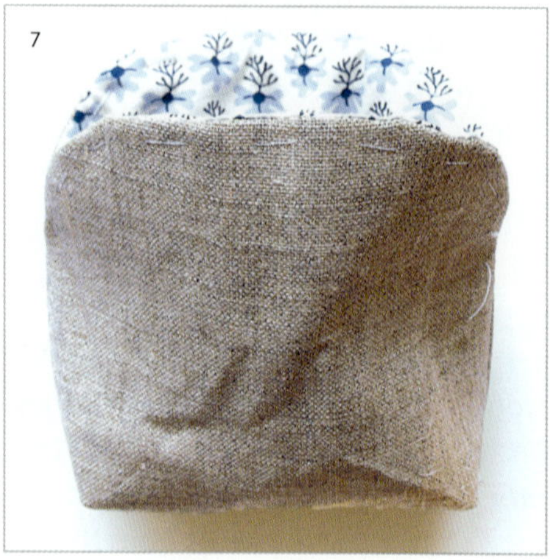

8

MAKEUP BAG (page 23)

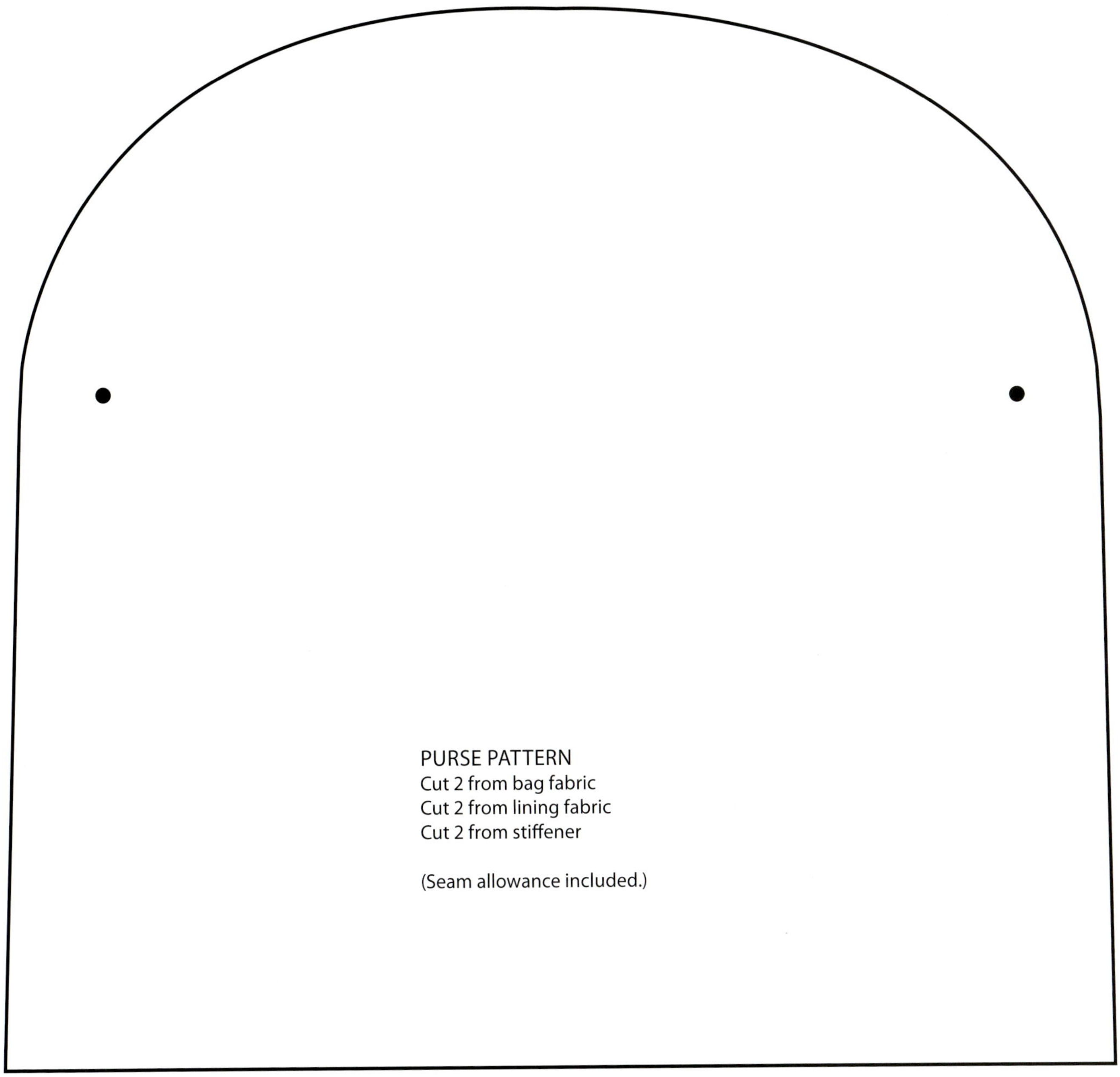

MAIN PHOTOS: EMMA NOREN; STEP-BY-STEP PHOTOS: JEMIMA SCHLEE

FUROSHIKI BAG

Furoshiki is a type of traditional Japanese wrapping cloth that was frequently used to transport clothes, gifts or other goods. Make a simple bag using this age-old technique.
By Jemima Schlee

YOU WILL NEED

- Two $15^3/4$" x $31^1/2$" rectangles of printed fabric
- 6" circular bamboo handles
- Sewing machine and thread
- Scissors
- Iron

TO MAKE

Note: *Match raw edges and use a $^1/2$" seam allowance unless otherwise indicated.*

1 Matching **wrong** sides and long edges, sew the rectangles together along one long edge. Trim one seam allowance to $^1/8$". Press the seam allowances toward the wider seam allowance. Fold the wider seam allowance in half over the trimmed seam allowance. Press both seam allowances to the opposite side so that both raw edges are hidden. Topstitch along the folded edge.

2 To hem fabric, fold all four sides in $^1/4$" and $^1/4$" again. Topstitch along folded edges.

3 To attach the handles, place the fabric right side down with the seam vertically in front of you. Place one handle at the bottom of the seam and pull the bottom corners through the handle from the front to the back (*image 1*).

4 Flip the handle up, pull the fabric corners to the front around the handle and knot the ends together, adjusting the fabric so it lies nicely and the knot ends are facing the outside. (*images 2 and 3*).

5 Repeat Steps 3 and 4 to attach the remaining handle (*image 4*).

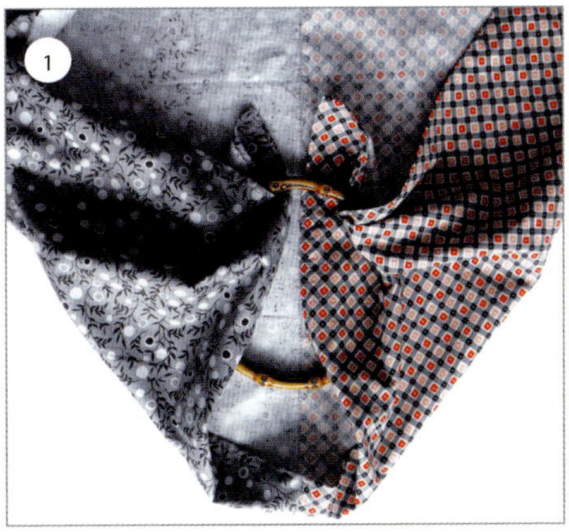

1

2

3

4

TIPS

- Furoshiki bags are traditionally made with silk headscarves or scraps of kimonos.
- To make a sturdier bag, simply stitch two $31^1/2$" squares of fabric together for a double-layer bag. Tie to the handles.

LAUNDRY BAG

Make sorting your laundry a breeze with our playful patterned bags.

by Francine Kay

PHOTO: RACHEL WHITING

YOU WILL NEED

Yardage is based on 43"/44" wide fabric with a usable width of 40".

- $3^{3}/_{8}$ yds of fabric for bag
- 12" x 12" square of fabric for appliqué
- $3^{3}/_{8}$ yds of ribbon for drawstring
- Fabric scissors
- Pins
- Sewing machine
- Safety pin (for threading ribbon through casing)

These drawstring laundry bags are ideal for separating whites, colors and delicates and you can customize them with your own appliqué designs to help tell them apart. We've used a cute T-shirt design. Choose bright fabrics for yours and add some cheer to your laundry room.

TIP

- To make your laundry bags more elaborate, you could decorate your T-shirt with rickrack, beads or buttons.

TO MAKE

***Note:** Match right sides and raw edges and use a $^{1}/_{2}$" seam allowance unless otherwise indicated.*

1 Cut out 2 rectangles of bag fabric each 40" x 59".

2 Enlarge the t-shirt pattern. Pin it to the appliqué fabric and cut around it with fabric scissors.

3 Position the appliqué on the lower end of one piece of the bag fabric; pin in place. Set the sewing machine to zigzag. Carefully sew around the appliqué.

4 Stopping 2" from the top on one side, sew the bag pieces together along side and bottom edges. Zigzag the seam allowances to prevent ravelling. Press the seam allowances 1/2" to wrong side at the unstitched area.

5 To make the casing for the ribbon, press the top edge of the bag 1/2" to wrong side and press 1"to wrong side again. Pin in place and machine stitch along the bottom folded edge.

6 To thread the ribbon through the casing, attach a safety pin to the ribbon and feed it through. Pull the ribbon to gather the bag and knot the ends.

LAUNDRY BAG (page 28)

Photocopy at 151% for actual size

MAIN PHOTOS: EMMA NOREN; STEP-BY-STEP PHOTOS: JEMIMA SCHLEE

DIP-DYED TOTE

Turn a simple linen sack into a stylish shopping tote.
By Jemima Schlee